Youth Marketing 101

I0472800

By

Graham Brown
Ghani Kunto
Freddie Benjamin

Graham Brown, Ghani Kunto, Freddie Benjamin

ACKNOWLEDGMENTS

Thank you to the Youth Marketing Academy students. Your stories and insights from all over the world helped made this book possible.

www.YouthMarketingAcademy.com

Introduction

Youth Marketing Ain't No Sprint

In his book "The Dip", Seth Godin wrote that no runner gives up on the Boston Marathon at the 25th mile mark. Statistically, the worst point for drop-out is the 13 mile half-way point, the point at which you're neither motivated by the excitement of the start nor within view of the finish line.

Think of this book as a coach to help you get through the race that is youth marketing. A benign dictator, if you will, shouting encouragement from the sidelines with a smile on its face as you get on your bike Sunday morning. We need encouragement because marketing is, let's face it, hard work. Marketing's hard work because it's a lot easier to sit on a couch watching TV, eat a bowl of nachos and worry about other people doing the running for us. We need encouragement because youth marketing today is forever at that 13-mile halfway point.

Talk to your ad agency and they'll pitch you the idea that youth marketing is the 100m dash: fun, exciting and sexy. Ad agencies take the pain away. Ad agencies are the ab-trainers on late night TV infomercials that seduce you with the promise of "getting ripped" for summer with only 30 minutes of exercise. It's the bank manager in a pair of jeans, girls in roller blades on campus, industry awards or Lady Gaga turning up at your product launch.

What I'd like to share with you in this book is, however, a different reality: *what works* and *what is commonly practiced* aren't two of the same. If advertising was so good, why don't ad agencies advertise? The reason is that youth marketing isn't Usain Bolt at the 100m; it's the harder, less glamorous slog of the Boston marathon.

For the last 50 years we've been practising the sprints. Our whole industry is based around short-term results (or "campaigns" to use the vernacular). We run out of puff after the first 10 minutes and wonder why the field is passing us, so we go back to the agency and beg for "the next big thing". It worked in the era of TV and the "Big Idea" but not today. Marketing needs to win customers not awards.

The economics of winning customers today means that success is determined not in your choices between "social" or "traditional" media or how you incorporate "social" into your advertising but in choices of mindset. A boring old bank using a print magazine to help young customers tell their story is far more relevant than an exciting mobile startup using social media to talk about its latest campaign or product launch. The overused maxim "the medium is the message" no longer applies: what counts is the mindset. That means moving from viewing youth as *destinations* for your marketing messages to treating them as *partners* in its production. This timeless truth holds true regardless of the medium you employ to convey the message. And when youth are your partners, it doesn't become a solo race anymore, it's a relay. They'll carry you across the finish line.

Lessons Learned on the Rocky Road to Youth Marketing Success

We easily forget that getting youth to buy your stuff is *very easy*. The real challenge is the gap between acknowledging youth's importance to your business and doing something about it. It's at this point youth marketers face a chasm of risk. It's easier to turn back and simply let others do the hard work but it doesn't help you next time round when you encounter the same challenges.

Youth marketing is a mindset not a strategy. You can't do "youth marketing" by hiring an agency to create a monkey-on-a-bike campaign for your Facebook page. Quick fixes land you right back where you started. What you need to cross is the right mindset, and that's what you'll get from this book.

Once you have the right mindset, you start asking the right questions. Once you start asking the right questions you avoid the potholes that knock you out of the race. When you stay in the race, you win the youth marketing game because your competitors inevitably drop out.

We discovered this simple truth to this game in our research that is the only strategy you have to know: **you win the youth marketing game by not losing**. Losing means capitulating and handing your marketing budget over to the creative agency because "you'll never get fired for booking a TV campaign." Losing is blowing your budget on a "Big Idea", wondering why it didn't work and then concluding that "youth are fickle / difficult to reach" or, worse still, "the only thing they understand is cheap."

Many of these mistakes are obvious and avoidable because the history of youth marketing is littered from them. You don't have to repeat these mistakes. You can learn from the successes and failures of 10+ years working with organizations like MTV, UNICEF, Nokia, Apple, Red Bull, Vodafone, Monster and Threadless. It's 10+ years of youth research and consultancy across 65 markets that we'll share in a nutshell in this book.

Curious

I'm hoping you're reading this book because you're curious.

You're curious about what's working today and what may be tomorrow. You're curious about what's the truth in marketing and what's hype. Our goal in writing this book has not been to quell your curiosity with a single bite-sized answer that "youth marketing is X" but to equip you with the right questions and tools to propel that curiosity on a journey of discovery.

Well, you've taken the first step. If you want the sprint, go buy a book about social media or the "secrets" of brand management.

This, however, is the marathon. But that doesn't mean it's going to need a Herculean effort to read this book. In contrast, you could devour this book in less time than it takes the average runner to run the marathon, all from the comfort of your armchair or airline seat (with or without nachos). Why complicate matters with a 200-page essay about social media when social media isn't the *main thing*? If we can provide you with the right tools and questions to address the main thing in 50 pages rather than 200, are you going to be disappointed? No, of course not. I'm hoping that, as with many of the ideas raised in this book, we'll save you precious time.

Youth Marketing 101 is just the beginning of a journey rather than the destination itself so I encourage you to join the Facebook Group (link provided at the end) to help you along. Like many of this book's readers, this book is going to raise more questions than it answers. If this is the case, we've succeeded in our goal.

Graham Brown

The Youth Marketing Academy

www.YouthMarketingAcademy.com

Part 1:

Timeless Marketing Truths

The Pepsi Challenge

Back in the 80s, Pepsi reached its zenith as a youth brand. Stealing market share from its rival infused the company with a growing sense of confidence. The company launched the "Pepsi Challenge," aimed to assert this upstart cola as the *de facto* youth brand of choice. In the Challenge, customers took blind taste tests and were asked to choose between Pepsi and Coke. 60% said Pepsi tasted better. In Pepsi's mind, the better product won out.

Researchers in the 90s repeated the Pepsi Challenge but employed a subtle twist. Rather than making the subjects wear blindfolds and drinking anonymous colas, they told the subjects which brands they were drinking *first*. The result? Four times as many people said they *preferred* the taste of Coke. Pepsi tasted better, but Coke had the better story. The simple marketing truth that is as relevant as it was in the 80s as it is today in the 21st century is as follows: youth don't buy *stuff*, they buy what *stuff* does *for* them.

Youth Don't Buy Stuff (Content), They Buy What Stuff Does For Them (Context)

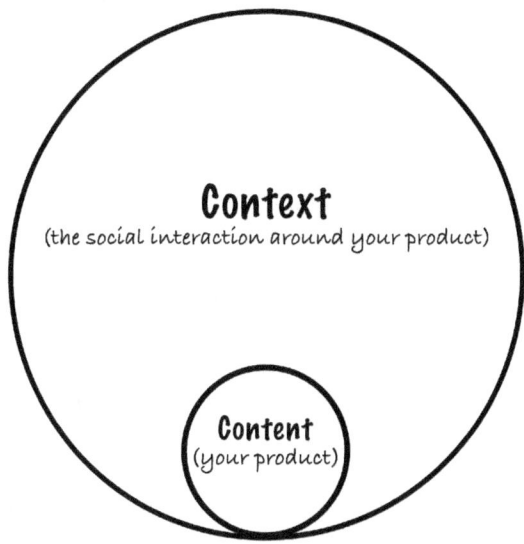

While companies sell products (Content) people actually buy the social package (Context). As Seth Godin pointed out, "blind taste tests are only good if you have blind customers," and "people drink the can not the soda." The can is the social packaging – the ability to use this product as a Social Tool, to help tell the customer's own story.

Don't Fall in Love with Your Product

Much of what we'll share in this book is about exploding the myths because as we've already mentioned, getting youth to buy the stuff is actually very easy. The challenge is the pitfalls that lie en route to the finish line like, for example, the myth that your product Content is any good. This may sound harsh but it's a refreshing taste of reality that will help you cast off any ideas you have about self-importance in the lives of your target customer.

The first step towards being a good youth marketer is understanding this difference between Content and Context. Call it humble pie. You live in a brand bubble whether you like it or not – you wake up thinking about that marketing meeting, product launch memos, emails to your creative agency and PR people. You wake up thinking about your brand, youth don't. Nobody cares about your product (like you do). And that's okay because great brands accept this truth and work within these new parameters. When the product manager tells you "but ours has 3x the memory" you know that you haven't even reached first base. When an agency runs a campaign highlighting the product's key features you need to ask yourself who is this benefitting – the agency or the customer? What they should be doing is emphasizing this product's benefits as a Social Tool. How will using this product help me belong? How will it help me be significant? Don't tell me that your youth "are different here". These are Universal drivers experienced by every youth in every country. Don't fall in love with your product, fall in love with what your product does for them.

What Marketers Think vs. Reality

	What marketers think	Reality
People buy...	Stuff	What stuff does for them
What's important?	Content	Context
A youth brand has to be...	Cool	Relevant
Good marketing is...	Award-winning, clever, funny, ad campaigns with celebrities with social media element	Helping youth tell their story and connect with each other

- Youth don't buy stuff, they buy what stuff does for them
- People drink the can not the soda
- Blind taste tests are only good if you have blind customers

Cigarettes vs. Mobile Phones

Why would people buy a product that killed them? It doesn't make sense. If people were really buying the Content of cigarettes, whole generations of young people would avoid the perils of tobacco. Young smokers know the health risks but the Context of cigarettes - the sense of belonging afforded among fellow smokers, the brand stories, the rituals of smoking, cigarette sharing – can be more important than life itself.

While youth smoking in general is declining, the need for the Context that the cigarette provided remains. Youth aren't suddenly becoming less social or less concerned about their importance in the Universe; they're turning to other forms of Content to offer similar Context those cigarettes once provided. Mobile phones check many of these boxes. At the level of Content, these two products are worlds apart but consider their Context. Consider the ritual, talking about phones, the camaraderie, the brand identities and the visual displays. When young people used to stand waiting for friends outside station exits they'd smoke a cigarette – they're virtual friend. Now they check imaginary text messages. A study by World Bank in Philippines shows purchasing a mobile phone led to a decrease of tobacco consumption by 32.6% in households. Data from mobileYouth also shows that, from late 1990's, the number of youth smokers in USA decreased as more young people purchased mobile phones. Content is interchangeable, the Context is not.

Mobile phones and cigarettes are Social Tools that offer similar Context: belonging, ritual, sharing, emancipation, and independence. When we stop thinking about our stuff as products and start thinking about it as a Social Tool we consider it in a new light. As a Social Tool it's a means to achieve a social end. When it's not the most effective tool out there, youth will replace it.

When we think about Social Tools we also think about whether we're selling the benefits of the Content or the Context: How will this help a young person to belong? How will this help a young person be significant?

Successful Brands Are Social Tools

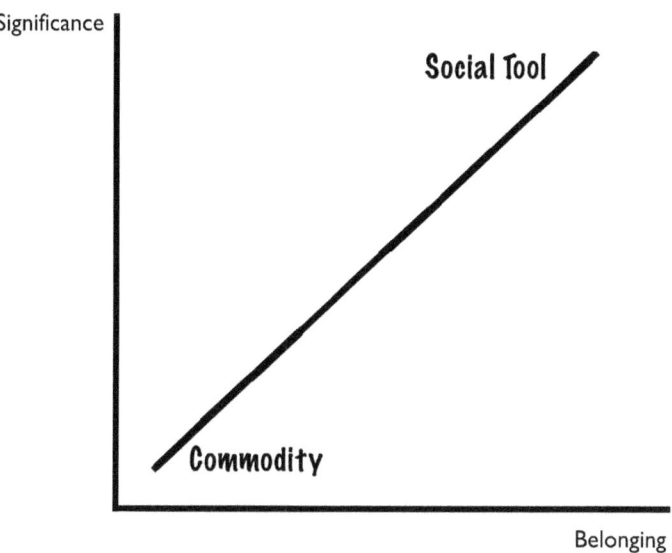

Our behavior is shaped by social needs - the most powerful of which is the drive for belonging and significance. We make choices based on these drivers that can appear irrational e.g.; buying a product that kills us. That's because we buy on emotion and justify with logic.

- Youth buy on emotion and justify with logic
- Social context can be more important than life itself

Content Is Interchangeable

	Cars	Cigarettes	Mobile Phones
Belonging	Give ride to friends, drive to friends house	Hang out with smokers, back of bus, same brand, ritual	Call, message, share photos, same brand, ritual, txtspk
Significance	Old enough to drive, independence, status symbol, knowledge	Old enough to smoke, rebellion, image of cool, knowledge	Old enough to own, independence, status symbol

Tools help us fulfill these social needs; a mobile phone can help us stay in touch with friends or be a status symbol. Mobile phones, however, are just one of many products that can fulfill these needs; seemingly unrelated products can also be competitors e.g. a car, a mobile phone and Lego bricks.

Comparison Of Content And Context

	Content	Context
What is it?	Product What we buy	Social Package Why we buy
Drivers	Logic	Emotion
Examples	Price, Touchscreen keyboards, Offer, Design	Need to belong Need to be significant
Marketing tools	Advertising, Campaigns, Sponsorship, Celebrities, PR	Communities, Social Programs, Events, Projects
Who creates it?	Companies	Users, customers, fans
Experience	Content experience starts after the purchase & exists only during direct interaction with the product.	Context experience starts before the purchase, exists even when not interacting with the product, lasts way beyond the end of product usage.

The Pepsi Generation

Pepsi understood the difference between Content and Context well. Pepsi knew that youth drank the can, not the soda. It was one of the first companies to employ storytelling in its marketing to help develop specific market segments. Pepsi was the first beverage brand to overtly target African Americans. It was also the first of its kind to depart from pushing the physical benefits (Content) of the product and start talking about lifestyle (Pepsi was originally a cure for Dyspepsia – a stomach condition). In 1963, advertising executive Alan Pottasch convinced Pepsi to move away from advertising these product features to highlighting the intangible benefit that had little to do with the product's medicinal origins. To Pottasch, the growing importance of media in teen lives presented an opportunity for advertising to play a bigger role in helping this lost generation find their voice. The Pepsi Generation was born.

Pepsi's invitation, "Come Alive! You're the Pepsi Generation!" helped young Baby Boomers growing up in post-war America find their place in the Universe. Not only did the message create a sense of belonging among teens, it also differentiated a whole generation from their parents. Where parents were concerned about the ever-present specter or war and loss, teens in the 50s and 60s sought to celebrate the moment through free time, consumerism and Rock'n'Roll.

Advertising created Context by telling stories that people identified with. Pepsi gave a lost generation a place in a rapidly changing world. Advertising also became headlines news (MTV Pepsi Generation Madonna 1989). Advertising gave us identity, conversation and we, the consumers, looked forward to seeing it on television.

Youth marketing has changed fundamentally within the last generation in 2 ways and we'll look at these 2 changes in section 2.

1) The New Attention Economy: The cost of youth attention has increased exponentially
2) Advertising is no longer the only way of creating Context

1) The New Attention Economy: The Cost of Youth Attention Has Increased Exponentially

Advertising's success, however, has been its own undoing; the model of "tell them you're cool, tell them in a big way and keep telling them" is one easily copied by any brand wanting to win consumer mindshare. It's a successful format easily translated to all media formats leading to an exponential rise in supply that outstripped demand (we only had 24 hours a day to give and 2 eyes and ears to consume it with.) When CPG brands recruited the best young blood from B-School the question they were continuously challenged with by these new upstarts was "how big will my marketing budget be?"

The game became less about creativity (that was outsourced to the agency) and all about the depth of your pockets. It was an era of "Go big or go home" and the "Big Idea". He who had the biggest ad budget won because he could afford the best ad agency, the most media space and the best celebrities to drown out the competition.

Cost of youth attention eventually hit a breaking point – a point at which it was no longer profitable to employ traditional marketing to reach youth. The average youth is already an expert at blocking advertising from even entering her field of consciousness. Of the small amount of messages that do reach her awareness, she trusts little. Less than 34% of American youth trust advertising. The average American will have seen 170,000 marketing messages by age 17. When you have a whole generation adept at filtering out these messages the whole marketing model changes. No longer can you simply buy youth trust and attention, you have to earn it. We'll cover these changes in **section 2 under Earned Media.**

The Cost of Youth Attention Is Increasing

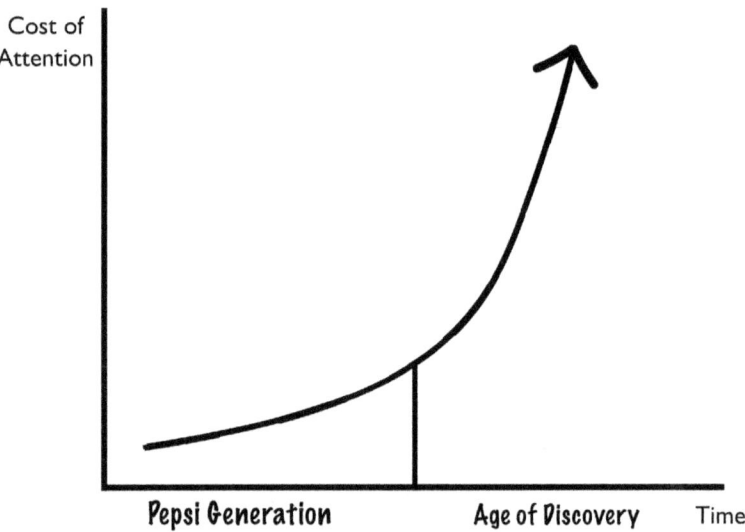

Cost of Attention

Pepsi Generation   **Age of Discovery**   Time

Today, when teens want to know about a brand, they ask each other, look up YouTube or search Google. Pepsi's TV advertising campaign is just one of many brand narratives happening right now. Digital media has also opened up storytelling, and the creation of context, to the customer.

2) Advertising is no longer the only way of creating Context

The cost of youth attention was expensive before digital arrived but it was digital that changed the game completely. Before digital, brands and advertising could control the storytelling because only those with money, knowledge and access could tell stories. Whether you liked, loved or loathed a product only your immediate circle knew about it. Today, however, everyone has access from the high school student posting reviews on Youtube to your worst critics on your Facebook fan page. Now they're all storytellers and it's out of your control.

The media formats may have changed but the mindset we use to reach youth is still the same old Paid Media model. The dynamics may have changed but the truth still holds true: People buy Context not Content. What has changed is who now creates the Context – the advertising agency or the customer?

We'll cover these changes in section 2 under **Fans.**

PART 2

The Change:
The Rise of Earned Media

South Africa's Coolest Brand

In June and July 2010, the eyes of the world turned to South Africa as it hosted the 19th World Cup Soccer tournament. Adidas and Coca Cola paid between $24 and $44 million for their annual fee to FIFA between 2007 and 2010 just to be able to call themselves an Official 2010 World Cup *Partner*. Other titles such as Official Sponsor and National Supporter were also available for an annual fee of $10 - 25 million and $4.5 - 7.5 million respectively. Nineteen companies bought the licenses, taking FIFA's tournament sponsorship revenues alone estimated to be around $250 million.

Despite the fact that the usual favorites Italy and France, along with the host country were all eliminated in the first round, the tournament continued to garner media attention and keep the advertisers happy. More than 700 million people watched the final game, making it one of the most watched events in the history of television. Even the lunar landing of 1969 had only 500 million viewers.

Did all this advertising pay off? Ten months later, the South African newspaper The Sunday Times announced the results of a survey of over 7,200 young South Africans in a study that spanned 72 categories of brands. The survey asked which was the coolest brand in South Africa. Surely, with the media coverage and awareness generated by the World Cup just passed, it would be down to one of either Coca Cola or Adidas? Not a chance. The winner wasn't an official World Cup Partner, Sponsor or Supporter. The *Coolest Brand Overall* in South Africa was BlackBerry.

Advertising might capture awareness but youth attention elsewhere. BlackBerry was winning the South African youth market not because of its advertising but because of its social Context. Blackberry messenger (BBM) was an effective tool for young South Africans to maintain discrete personal networks outside of work, email and parents. It's the same social Context behind its success in markets like Indonesia, Thailand, and India. Blackberry wasn't Adidas or Coke, it was "your dad's phone." Blackberry was popular because it inferred the owner with a sense of arrival, that they by owning this executive toy had somehow "made it". Now, this doesn't mean that "being cool" is about following what their dads are doing – that would be a real disaster. What brands shouldn't be doing is thinking about "cool" in the first place but thinking more about relevance. The challenge for every youth marketer is figuring out the drastic shifts of today's landscape of social Context and going beyond *what's normally practiced* and looking at *what really works*. What really works is understanding the individual stories young people tell about themselves using these products, not the official monolithic brand narrative from the agency.

What young South Africans think about their BlackBerry:

"South Africans love BB's. In a college class of 250, 70 use BlackBerries with 67 of those being 8520 Curve."
Hackson

"Proud to be South African and use a BlackBerry :) if only we'd get the 9900 the same time as overseas and not wait 3 - 5 months once it's been launched."
Ari 79

"i totally AGREE!!!!!!!! i loove my blackberry im 17 and im obsessed with it! me and my friends comunicate trough BBM all the time!!! and we also have a twilight fanclub and we all can cordinate activities and chat trough our BBM group! blackberry its the perfect device for anyone who has an active social life!!! and bussines life!!!!!!! I ♥ BLACKBERRY!!!!!!!"
alexrocks502

From Liked to Loved

As The Beatles said, "can't buy me love." Advertising gets people to "like" you, but recommendation creates real brand "love". Advertising is about getting elected – finding a story that offends the least and is acceptable by the most. Back then, it worked. Because Pepsi could afford the $25m for Michael Jackson's endorsement, every Pepsi ad became one big testimonial, "we can afford MJ because kids like you are buying our soda" but real brand "love" today comes from whether or not that brand lets youth tell their story. You can't build a brand on fake product reviews. You can't build a brand by forcing youth to talk about your product. Youth talk about your product when it allows them to talk about themselves. This is the key distinction between Paid (advertising, media buys, social media campaigns) and Earned (recommendation, word of mouth) media. Earned media is just that, *you can't buy it*.

Comparison Of Paid And Earned Media

	Paid Media	**Earned Media**
What is it?	Advertising, sponsorship, endorsements	Word of mouth
Impact	Short term awareness	Long term recommendation
How do you control it?	Brand management	Brand democracy
Who creates it?	Brand	Customers (Fans)
How do you get it?	Buy it (media space)	Earn it

The whole marketing model was built on a time when youth truth and attention were abundant; that simply isn't true anymore. Now, we have access to more trusted media e.g. friends via social media, Google etc. Although advertising is still able to achieve 'top of mind', awareness and drive brand recall it isn't the most important influence on final purchase decision.

T-Mobile's Flashmob

15 January 2009, Liverpool Station, London. The day went as would any other Thursday when the music started playing at 11am. Four hundred seemingly random people broke into a choreographed dance routine to a medley of hip-hop, disco. Early morning commuters who were not part of it looked on with a bewildered smile. Some tried to join in. Hidden cameras all over the station captured the moment. The footage was edited, packaged, debuted the next day on Youtube to widespread industry acclaim as a "brave" move by a mobile operator into the world of social.

T-Mobile's "Life is for Sharing" flashmob campaign created buzz. More than 33 million people viewed it on YouTube. Many thought the ad cool, clever and fun. The creative agency behind the "Big Idea", Saatchi & Saatchi, won the 2009 British Television Advertising industry's award for "best advertising campaign."

"Life is for Sharing" was not the only reason T-Mobile received a lot of attention that year. 2009 was a year of peak attrition with more customers leaving the network to join rivals than ever. The cause? T-Mobile's competition didn't have better advertising; they invested more in what worked. As one viewer commented, "In the few seconds it had my attention I was suddenly unable to move away from the screen & honestly I have been searching on the Internet for it since. But whatever, I'm not going to change my network because of it." The $1.5 million ad campaign could have been better spent on customer service, front line staff or better billing systems but, as is often the case of great youth marketing failures, we end up outsourcing the creativity to an agency more concerned with winning awards than winning customers. Welcome to the marathon. The marathon means investing in the unsexy stuff like the customer experience. It won't win you awards but it will grow your business.

That year T-Mobile's parent company, Deutsche Telekom, reported its mobile division had lost $849 million and wrote down a further $2.4 billon. Advertising today may not only be ineffective it may also be detrimental to your business. No matter how much you spend on advertising, or how memorable or viral you've made it, you can't buy customer's trust, you have to earn it. Spending money on advertising means not spending money on what counts. Young people simply don't wake up thinking about your brand anymore so why try and change that? The Big Idea, even with a social spin, is over. This is the dawn of a new era, the era of Earned Media.

While marketing may acknowledge the Big Idea is broken, it's difficult for the marketing industry change. As long as the metrics that measure marketing success (i.e. top of mind, awareness etc.) remain unchallenged, activity will continue to yield the same results. A social media campaign will still focus on using Facebook for being *liked* or YouTube for the number of views whereas real influence happens when a customer who *loves* a product recommends it to a friends, for free. Adding social media to the mix isn't going to change anything, it simply patches over the cracks (and in some cases makes it worse.)

Real change means changing the metrics first: moving from liked to loved, from paid to earned media and from vanity metrics to recommendation.

- Is your marketing winning awards or winning customers?
- If youth like your brand be afraid, be very afraid.
- You can't buy youth trust and attention anymore, you have to earn it.

Youth Don't Care About Your Brand

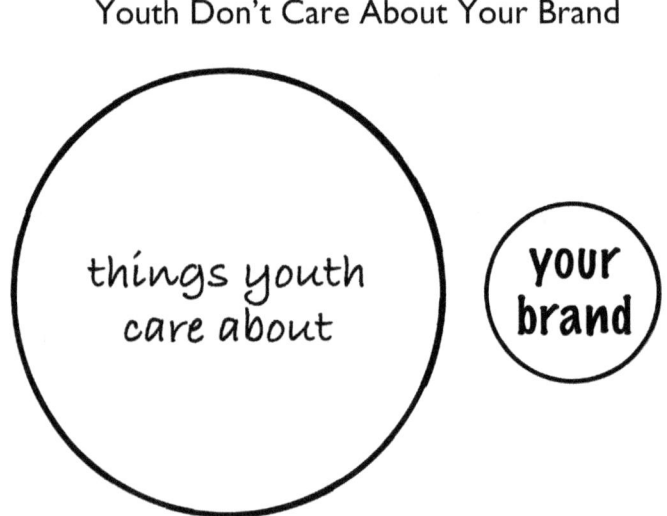

Lego Fans

For a product that's nothing more than colorful plastic bricks, it's amazing to think about the number of Lego fans out there and how passionate they are about the brand. Do a search for "brickfilm" on YouTube and you'll find 23,000 entries of stop-motion films that took hours to create. Go on Flickr and search for "Lego" and you'll find more than 1.3 million pictures of Lego bricks arranged to create scenes from Harry Potter to Lord of the Rings. At first glance it's just a plastic brick. On second, it's a Social Tool. That's how these seemingly valueless product can survive and thrive in a world of iPads, Wiis and online entertainment.

Lego fans are people like Kevin Walter who built a 2-meter high replica of Sauron's tower, Barad Dur, from the book and movie Lord of the Rings. Reporting on the story, magazine RegHardware writes "some people have too much time on their hands." But that's one of the defining characteristics of a Fan: unlike customers, fans always find the time to indulge their passions. These aren't the easy-come-easy-go fans you get on Facebook. Fanning a Facebook Page means nothing so making that your campaign goal is a waste of time. Real fandom is a labor of love. It's a labor because it costs time, money and effort. Lego fans attend Legocons, spend hours online playing games like Minecraft, find time to talk to other Fans. Lego Fans have made the conscious decision to mix with likeminds and, therefore, mix less with others. You don't become a Fan by clicking a button, you become fan by investing your personal story into a brand. If Fans simply "liked" the product it would be lost in those 170,000 marketing messages. Kevin Walter doesn't care what those around him think because this interest economy – a connected diaspora of passions – is no longer a compromise of second-bests or least-worsts.

For many "customers," building a tower out of 50,000 bricks and 2 months of your life is too geeky, too nerdy to consider. But for Kevin, it's not just a passion; it's also that Social Tool. The tower involved 15 people from different countries all who pitched in ideas and designs to aid the construction. They shared their ideas on the website Mocpages - a home for Lego fans to share their passions - under the project entitled "The Journey of the Fellowship" (referencing the whole Lord of the Rings saga) from Inn of the Prancing Pony complete with slate roof tiles to the fellowship's journey through the Mines of Moria. Each was created with love.

Lego Supports the Fans

Lego knows that from the 100,000 views Kevin aggregated on his Flickr stream of Barad-Dur, and the numerous meetups, and interest groups Kevin participates in with fellow enthusiasts, that offline social interaction - not plastic bricks - is why they do it. Sure, there are cheaper bricks out there and they more or less look the same. Why pay twice the price for Lego? It's here that brands learn what their business is really about. Being social is not about getting on social media, it's about helping your fans be social. Lego doesn't crack down on Legocons for bearing the official Lego logo or prevent its employees from communicating with these Fans. It actively encourages connection not just between the Fans but also between Fans and the employees (who are also Fans who just happened to be working there.) If a print magazine can help connect Lego fans with each other it's more "social media" than a Facebook fan page that talks about the latest product launch. This connection doesn't happen in the virtual world. You can't fake it with an online community. The end result has to be where real meaning is created, offline. Your fans may already be meeting each other in self-organized conventions. How are you supporting it? Where are you in this conversation?

The Interest Economy

We live in an era of Fans. Some of us grew up in an era where Fans had to compromise. If you were a Lego fan, you'd hope that those in your immediate neighborhood and school year were also Lego fans else you risk being outcast and bullied. Most would suck it up; play along with the mass. Today, however, Fans can indulge in their fantasies to their hearts' content. They don't have to compromise their fandom, they can connect with other fans just like them around the world. The fan neighborhood is global, not your real world neighbor but like Mocpages.

Inside every customer is a fan and every brand has fans. You might not notice them because you're still using the Loudspeaker Model: your own brand message - advertising, branding campaigns, etc. - is drowning them out. It's a defunct model. Think of youth marketing today not as the Loudspeaker but the Telephone: you need to connect all these digital Diasporas and help them have a conversation with each other (not with your brand). Youth marketing is about connecting the dots of the Interest Economy. The best way you can "be a part of the conversation" (to use the agency vernacular) is to facilitate it rather than be it. When you phone a friend, your conversation isn't prefaced by a message from the mobile network telling you what you need to talk about. We know what to talk about. We do this everyday, without prompt. What youth need help with is the tools to make that conversation happen.

Loudspeaker vs. Telephone Model Of Customer Experience

	Loudspeaker Model	Telephone Model
Brand Story	Singular, monolithic, manufactured	Multiple, individual, organic
Relationship w. brand	Liked	Loved
Customers are...	Destinations	Partners
Focus	Customers	Fans
Who controls brand narrative?	Agency	Fans

Loudspeakers vs Telephones:
Traditional vs Modern Youth Marketing

Loudspeaker Model

Telephone Model

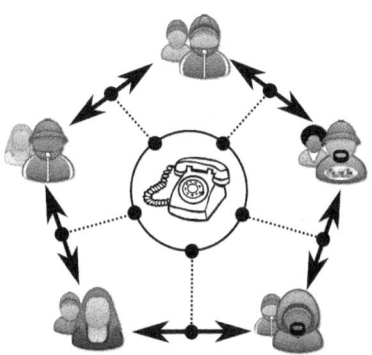

Loudspeaker vs. Telephone Model Of Marketing Strategy

	Loudspeaker Model	Telephones Model
Model	One-to-Many	Many-to-Many
Media Access	Limited and controlled	Open and democratic
Success Factor	Biggest ad budget	Give voice to youth
Media Model	Paid Media	Earned Media
Media Tactics	fun/clever/smart ad campaigns	WOM, recommendation
Key Measurements	Awareness, reach, brand equity, market share, 'top of mind'	Earned Media Indexes, Net Promoter Score, Share of customer
Mindset	Brand Management (Control)	Brand Democracy (Curation)

Before digital, marketing was based on the economics of scarcity; limited shelf space, TV channels, billboards and advertising slots between programs. When resources are scarce, control is key to winning the game - from buying media space that crowds out competitors to producing the least offensive, most liked brand story that reaches everyone. Digital has changed the game 2 ways:

1) Abundance:

Customers no longer need to compromise their tastes, opinions and decisions. Geography is no longer a barrier, there's a group of people out there who love Lego just like you. Why settle for vanilla when you can have Rocky Road ice cream?

2) Tools:

Now, customers have a platform for their previously unheard voices. Customers can create their own brand narratives on YouTube, reviews products from Amazon's seemingly limitless array of options and text reviews of movies from inside the theater.

Liberated by an abundance of choice and armed with tools to tell their story - from Lego enthusiasts to fans of Korean pop in the US, digital is enabling an explosion in communities of mutual interest. Controlling the brand narrative is now not only ineffective but also detrimental especially for the next generation of customers who are growing up in the Interest Economy, unfettered by compromise and unafraid of exclusion.

The challenge for brands is moving away from a model in which they've become very proficient - from *creating* Context to *curating* it. How can an ad agency tell a more relevant, more authentic story about Lego than Kevin Walter? Who will Kevin's friends listen to more? Rather than compete with these numerous narratives, brand marketing needs to nurture these voices and create a platform for them to share. Nobody wants a dialogue with your brand; they want a dialogue with each other.

- Find your fans, the rest is mere detail
- Nobody wants a dialogue with your brand; they want a dialogue with each other

Part 3

Marketing in the Age of Earned Media

Trevor Moran

When Trevor Moran hit the Apple Store on Fifth Avenue New York in the Christmas of 2009 he wasn't like the thousands of customers who regularly beat the path to find the latest MacBooks and iPhones, looking for presents for the holiday season. Trevor was looking to record the latest episode in his story.

Trevor is better known as iTr3vor. More than 630,000 people subscribe to his official YouTube channel, with his most popular videos fetching from 100,000 to 1.5 million views. Since he was 12 years old, Trevor has been dancing and freaking out in front of the in-store MacBook webcam as bemused customers and staff look on. One week it's to the backbeat of Lady Gaga's "Telephone" next it's LFMAO's "Sexy and I Know It." Some customers ignore Trevor with a wry smile, "oh, it's that crazy kid again." Some join in for the hell of it. Trevor records his performance and uploads them to his YouTube channel. It's a routine he's kept up for more than 3 years.

Lego gave Kevin Walter tools. Apple also provides a Social Tool – a Social Space that helps Fans like Trevor speak to their followers and tell their stories. Trevor never records his dances at Best Buy or on a Dell laptop, but he's also no Apple *fanboy*; he rarely recommends Apple products directly. iTr3vor is all about Trevor, not about Apple or any other brands, and that's what makes him unique and authentic. The key to any youth marketing strategy is in knowing and helping your fans tell *their* stories. The rest is mere detail.

Fans are often youth with passion, sometimes extreme, always unsatiated. In Trevor's case, it's the silver screen. He's a wannabe actor and Apple is the vehicle for him to achieve his personal and social goals. Apple isn't a product, it's a step up to his life ambitions. That's *real* brand loyalty. Could this happen at Best Buy? Maybe, if they knew who their Fans were. Would employees allow it to happen, or would they try to shut him down?

The last question is particularly indicative of how great brands aren't the product of great strategies. Does the brand actively encourage a culture of participation at the frontline, or does it see iTr3vor as a nuisance? The results have little to do with agencies or the departments that look after branding or marcomms. The results of these actions have, however, a significant impact on the brand.

Great brands are the product of great culture. Brand Management is a culture of control, a culture of the Loudspeaker. Brand Democracy is a culture of curation and of the Telephone.

Fans: Not All Customers Are The Same

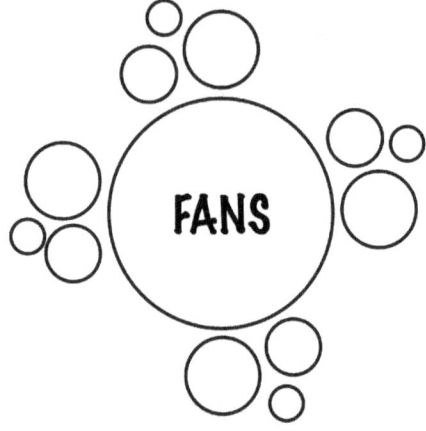

◯ customer segment
size of circle = size of influence

62% of youth bought mobile handsets (according to mobileYouth) based on what their friends not what the ad agency said. Within those friends are a core group of influencers – the 10% that influence the 90%. Fans aren't 2 or 3 times more influential than your average customer, they can be up to 100 times more influential. Not all customers are the same. Fans are also key partners in the customer experience from co-creating innovation to peer-to-peer customer service.

- If you don't know who your Fans are you have only customers
- It's not who's telling your story but whose story you're telling that counts

Comparison: Customers vs. Fans

	Customers	**Fans**
% of market	90%	10%
% of word of mouth	10%	90%
Relationship to brand	Like	Love
Character	Follower	Leader
How do they find out?	Through Fans	Through Early Adopters
Contribution to brand	Buy product	Marketing, Innovation, Customer Service and buy product
How do you reach them?	Through Fans	Break down the walls that prevent Fans from reaching you

Engaging Fans:

There are 3 steps to engaging Fans effectively:

- Choose Mindset

- Understand Their Motivations

- Let Go

1. Choose Mindset:

Moving from Brand Management to Brand Democracy means helping each Fan tell their individual story and marketing *with* not *to* them. The Loudspeaker model of marketing *to* customers alienates Fans by drowning out their story. An agency exec once proclaimed excitedly to me after an industry presentation that, "we'll be the Loudspeaker attached to your Telephone." Sometimes, the Loudspeaker just doesn't want to die. Even if you use the Loudspeaker to tell the Fans' story, you're still drowning the others out.

One of the key challenges faced in transition is the 90-10 rule. In Loudspeaker youth marketing you're focused on maximum awareness. Again, it's getting elected by the masses rather than being meaningful to the few. When you suggest that marketing should focus more on the 10% the initial resistance is "we can't build a business around a small group of customers." Well, the reality is that most brands are building a business around no customers. The 10% influence the 90%. The 90% aren't listening to you anyway. So what are you going to do? Simply throw the marketing budget into a big black hole of awareness? Great brands like Apple, Ford, Monster, Red Bull and Threadless all started with a small Beachhead of Fans and took it from there.

2. Understand Their Motivations:

If you don't know who your Fans are, you have only customers. Fans aren't "early adopters" – this is an easy mistake to make. They aren't necessarily the "cool kid" hipsters who camp outside Apple stores. Fans are people who love your product and they come in all different shapes and sizes. Each has their own unique personal motivation. Each brand has its own Fans, most just haven't found them yet. They still think about "customers".

Traditional research creates segmentation based around behaviors (e.g. what they bought) whereas Immersion looks at the "why" question behind those behaviors (e.g. why did they buy it?). Using Immersion research, brands can build Pen-Profiles of Fans to help understand the emotion rather than the logic of consumer behavior based on customer responses. See the example Pen-Profiles based on individual drivers, stories and aspirations below.

Example Of Fan Pen-Profile

Storyteller	Context (My story)	Social Currency (How brand helps me tell my story)	Shared Experience (Where my story takes place)
iTrevor	Budding movie producer	Create movies, share online, followers	Dancing in Apple stores
Kevin Walter	Lego enthusiast	Original creations,	Fan conventions, online communities

3. Let Go:

Allow Fans to do what they do naturally. Support their creative capacity and social needs to connect. Brands get in the way.

What Great Companies Do

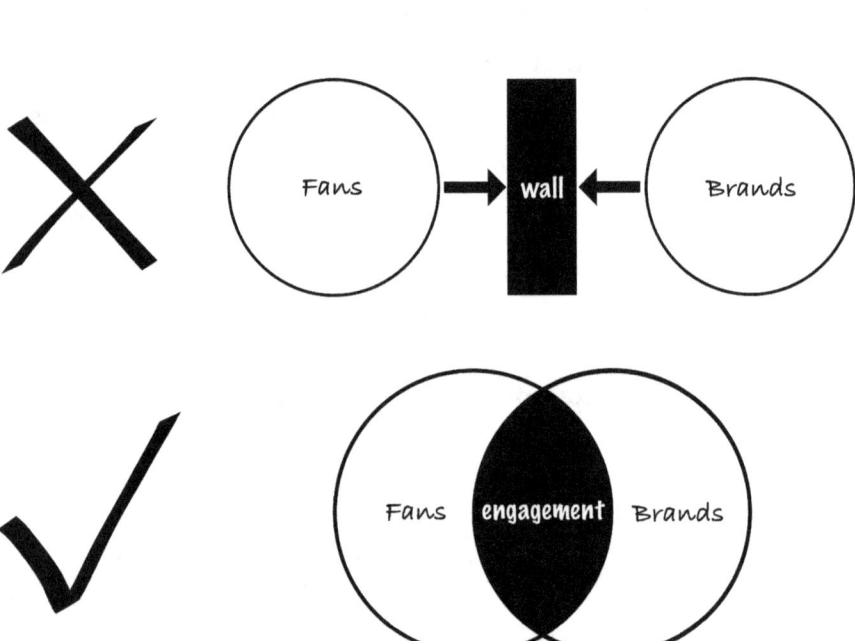

Advertising, product research & development and customer service call centers all are increasingly expensive cost centers within the business. When companies try to maintain control over customer experience, they unnecessarily internalize the costs.

Now, customers have the tools to be able to help each other, market or innovate the product - brands need to get out of the way. Companies that 'let go' and curate customer activity are able to spread these costs across the market because Fans do this stuff naturally. By letting Trevor Moran use Apple stores to tell his story,

Apple reduces marketing costs and gains Earned Media. In the Telephone model of youth marketing, cost centers become assets.

- Are you marketing *to* or marketing *with*?
- We need to move from viewing youth as destinations for our marketing messages to treating them as partners in its production.
- Rather than asking, "how do engage youth?" we should be asking, "how do we break down the walls that prevent youth from engaging us?"

Ford Fiesta Movement

Choosing a mindset, understanding your fans, and letting go sounds simple, especially if you're a company that was built with the right DNA. For companies entrenched in the old ways of doing things it might take new blood to bring about change and even then change needs to happen in slow increments. Take small steps and as long as your direction is correct, you'll steer the whole company towards a better direction. Ford is a great example of this.

Ford's brand's problems didn't lie in having a poor product line but in the long-term alienation of its Fans. Employees drove Ford. Employee families and friends drove Ford. Employees lived in towns where everyone either drove the brand or worked for a company that supplied it. When young people started buying cooler Japanese marques, Ford couldn't understand why its brand was suddenly uncompetitive. By 2008, stock price fell to $1.50 - around

5% of its value 10 years earlier. Ford was finished long before the recession ever hit.

How, then, did Ford go from being at the precipice of bankruptcy in 2008 to launching one of the top 10 coolest auto brands in 2011 in USA? The soon-to-be-launched Ford Fiesta wasn't received as some boring Japanese wannabe but a widely acclaimed game changer by domestic press. Bear in mind that this was a small engine sub-compact car in a market that has had a long love affair with SUVs, trucks and oversized sedans.

Ford's turnaround stemmed from its ability to identify and co-create with Fans, particularly American students who were already sold on the brand. The well worn track of building buzz, inviting journalists & celebrities, buying spots on TV, product placement in movies and autoshow reveals would have been to easy to follow. Rather than try to impress them with cool marketing campaigns, Ford realized that students had a lot to offer – from their ideas about fuel efficiency in the face of rising oil prices to the future roadmap for mobile phone / car integration. By creating a movement – the Ford Fiesta movement – Ford began to treat youth as partners as partners in the whole process. Sure, students couldn't actually design new models but they could help co-create the stories around the cars and share innovative ideas about in-car entertainment or safety.

"We didn't want A-list celebrities. We know that people trust people like themselves most, and our agents are a good representation of many of the people we're interested in reaching. Plus, they all *wanted* to be part of this - we didn't have to go out and hire them," said Scott Monty, Head of Social Media for Ford Motor Company.

Ford extended an open invitation to find young people who would be interested in borrowing a Fiesta for six months. At the end of the six months, one of them would receive a brand new Ford Fiesta. Over 4,000 people applied to become part of the Fiesta Movement. Ford accepted 100 of them and made them "Agents."

Ford followed their everyday stories, curated the content and gave it a home online. Agents created video shorts, documented their travels, discovered little-known places, interviewed interesting people - one of them even used the car to elope. Very few of the pictures taken and videos created were about the Fiesta itself. Those that did just showed the car briefly - around 3 seconds in a 5-minutes video. If it was Brand Management, the Loudspeaker and the Big Idea it would all be about Ford but the Agents weren't asked to talk about the car or the brand, they asked them to talk about themselves. In fact if you look at the agents' page on the Ford Fiesta Movement website you struggle to see any evidence of the Ford logo or brand. It wasn't about the car, after all. It was about the people. If it was Brand Management it would be "can you make the logo bigger?"

Ford didn't even ask the Agents to put their videos on the Fiesta Movement webpage; because these students were the type that loved to perform anyway (talk, write, act, sing, create movies) it was second nature. These hopefuls needed Ford's platform to tell their story and Ford needed them to generate the Earned Media it required to shape their target market. It was an approach that required a degree of confidence in the new Earned Media model and a departure from the ubiquitous "go social" attitude offered by creative agencies.

"The whole process has been very organic, warm and fuzzy, and not at all pushy or forced," said Maria De Los Angeles, Agent#27. "I'm not a 'money' person and I have no idea if this will help Ford's bottom line in the end when it comes to selling cars but I can tell you that from professional perspective that this has got to be one of the most brilliant campaigns ever. It fully engages us as ambassadors without us being hardcore sales people. We are not required to yap about the Fiesta constantly and we can pretty much say whatever we want. The only thing we're not allowed to do in our videos is shoot something stupid — i.e., driving without a seat belt, that sort of thing. Ford took a great risk in putting these cars in our hands."

Ford gave them a stage, a Social tool, a car for half a year and helped them do what they've always loved doing.

The Fiesta Movement was not an overnight success. The program started long before the first car hit the dealerships. What Ford was able to do was prime the market, identify the Fans and reduce the risk of a cold-start come launch day. Behind the scenes, Ford also opened up other opportunities for co-creation. University hackathons much like those hosted by Facebook challenged students to develop the kind of driving apps they wanted to see in their own cars. The best apps were taken forward (official or not) for in-car development, such as the SyncML Spotify app that allows the driver to play streaming music straight out of the car speakers from his or her Spotify playlist. Not only was this co-creation great innovation, it was also great marketing. The product development department was also the market.

The Evolution Of Ford's Youth Marketing

	How Ford Did It	How Ford Fiesta Does It
Marketing	Hire best ad agency to create brand story about car. Celebrity. Discounts and cash backs.	Invited Fans to help tell their own stories. Curated content on their Movement platform.
Innovation	Internal product development. Hire designers and design agencies to makeover car.	Organized Hackathons on campus. Supported "unofficial" in-car app development
Customer Service	Centralized, managed by dealers. Managing complaints and negative PR.	Community management. Encourage transparency. Facilitated interaction between customers.

Ford's Fiesta Movement is a departure from traditional auto youth marketing. Rather than develop a brand through campaigns, Ford chose a long term, organic approach of building a Permission Asset - a platform - to house youth conversation. Ford used new media to help Fans tell their story.

Ford's Beachhead approach has 3 distinct business benefits:

- Primed market before launch

- Shared risk of innovation and marketing with customers

- Created a feeder of ideas for innovation and marketing that could be assimilated into higher end brands within portfolio (e.g. F-series truck range)

Facebook - The Hacker Way

Chris Putnam was just your average college student who enjoyed playing average dorm room pranks. Using some basic code and a few CSS rewrites, he created an app that allowed people to see their Facebook pages but with a MySpace theme. You wouldn't normally give it much attention, except when Putnam received an email in his inbox from Facebook's co-founder Dustin Moskowitz.

There was a precedent to this.

One hacker before Kevin had tried a similar stunt on MySpace itself, which resulted in a probing email from the company's inner circle. After an exchange of emails, the wannabe hacker was invited to MySpace with the promise of a job offer only to find a group of cops waiting to arrest him at LAX airport.

Needless to say, Putnam was cautious. And it's here that youth marketing and innovation become culture not strategy. Here's Putnam's account of the message received from Facebook:

"His knowledge of my identity didn't come as much of a surprise since the worm's interaction with my account was a dead giveaway and we even went out of our way to provide contact information in the source code and CSS file. I'm having a hard time finding the exact text of his message right now, but it was along the lines of 'Hey, this was funny but it looks like you are deleting contact information from users' profiles when you go to replicate the worm again. That's not so cool.' This then led to a lot of back-and-forth between myself and Dustin where I explained the worm in detail and other holes I had found and planted worms within. He was incredibly friendly about the whole thing and we continued talking fairly frequently over AIM for a month or so. I pulled a couple more dumb stunts during this time, in particular locking up several college databases testing SQL injection holes."

Their relationship grew. In time, Moskowitz offered Putnam a job but rather than pulling the MySpace ambush at the airport, he ended up working in the Facebook development team. Putnam went on to work on the creation of a video sharing application which is now usable by all members today.

Facebook could have so easily copied MySpace and arrested Putnam but it chose not to because it was a group of young hackers like Putnam who made Facebook in the first place. When Putnam hacked Facebook, MySpace was the bigger of the two entities (300m vs. 150m accounts). MySpace today, however, is toast. It's toast not because of poor innovation or marketing strategies, but because of culture.

Chris Putnam's story is not a unique as you might think. Companies that understand Earned Media are companies that embrace the Telephone Model, and this means embracing your Fans, whoever they might be. Sometimes this means you have to embrace hackers. Nicholas Allegra (aka Comex) for example had released three JailbreakMe codes that basically cracked open the lock Apple had placed in its iPhones. Apple's response? Hired him as an intern. Sometimes it means co-creating with young people whose default approach to your product is "how can I break this to make it a better?" Either way, by letting go you end up with a more effective Social Tool.

Comparison Of Approach: MySpace vs. Facebook

	MySpace	Facebook
Culture	Develop internally, prosecute hackers, control source code	Encourage hackers, hire them (e.g. Chris Putnam), organize Hackathons
Growth	Rapid expansion: 9 months to reach 1 million (compared to 18 months for Facebook)	Organic: Built on initial Beachhead of college students (Harvard Alumni) before expanding to new markets
Content	Recruited and promoted celebrities, emphasized cool people	Everyone

Companies like Apple and Facebook get how youth marketing works. "Getting it" is not a strategy, it's a function of your corporate culture. As Facebook filed a prospectus for a five billion dollar initial public offering, CEO Mark Zuckerberg explained in a letter to potential investors about the company's culture he dubbed "The Hacker Way". Key to keeping this culture alive is the hackathons they organize every few months, where the whole team gets together and looks at everything that has been built. "Many of our most successful products came out of hackathons," Zuckerberg wrote, "including Timeline, chat, video, our mobile development framework and some of our most important infrastructure like the HipHop compiler."

The company extended The Hacker Way to its recruitment process. Go to Facebook's Career's page and you'll find the Programming Challenge. If you can solve programming challenges, you'll get a phone interview. It's a culture that's welcoming to change. It's a culture makes the company itself into a platform for Fans to tell their stories. Facebook has gone beyond creating a Permission Asset for its Fans and turned the company itself into a Permission Asset.

Facebook's success proves that youth marketing isn't about what you do but who you are. Two similar products can experience very different outcomes as a result of the choices they made about who they were and how they treated their customers, not the "Big Ideas" they had about marketing and innovation. You can't fake culture. You can't fix your culture by hiring in a creative agency to makeover the desk space.

3 Core Tenets of Facebook's Approach:

- Move fast and break things

- Done is better than perfect

- The riskiest thing is to take no risks

Next Steps

Join The Facebook Group

What's iTr3vor doing now?

How do you measure Earned Media?

How do you compete with a brand like Red Bull *and win*?

Why is a shoe company, Converse, building a music studio for its Fans?

How is Lego successfully curating its Fan community?

How is KFC Indonesia capturing the youth market by becoming a record label?

Can mobile co-creation improve the lives of African youth?

What are the five common mistakes banks make in youth marketing?

Why should brands fire their creative agencies?

Here's your opportunity to join the Youth Marketing Academy group for Youth Marketing 101 readers:

https://www.facebook.com/groups/yomaca/

Note: The Academy Group is invite-only. Have your book ready. We'll ask you a challenging but fun question about what you've just read. If you're answer the secret question successfully, you're in.

About the Authors

Graham Brown has spent his life living and working in both London and Tokyo. A psychology graduate, Graham has focused his career on understanding what influences consumer behavior. He has published 3 marketing books on Amazon.

As well as speaking at industry conferences on the subject of young consumers, Graham has appeared on CNBC, Sky News, CNN and BBC as well as in print with the FT, The Guardian, Wall Street Journal and The Sunday Times. Graham is also a panel judge for the Mobile Marketing Association and social media / youth board adviser to UNICEF.

Freddie Benjamin is the Research Manager at mobileYouth. He has prior experience in research and analysis of consumer behavior from US and Asia markets. He masters quantitative and qualitative research methods, design and ethnographic research. He is the co-author of the four-part mobileYouth report.

Ghani Kunto has been involved in the world of youth marketing and education since 2007. He hosts a number of business talk shows in television and radio. Ghani runs workshop on marketing in various countries in Asia. He currently teaches Consumer Behavior for Asian Banking Finance Institute in Jakarta, Indonesia